The VOCATION *of the* CATECHIST

Inspiration and Professional Growth

IMPRIMATUR

✝ Most Reverend
Robert J. McManus, STD,
Bishop of Worcester,
June 26, 2017

TWENTY-THIRD PUBLICATIONS
1 Montauk Avenue, Suite 200, New London, CT 06320
(860) 437-3012 » (800) 321-0411 » www.twentythirdpublications.com

Cover photo: ©iStockphoto.com / FatCamera

ISBN: 978-1-62785-287-6
Library of Congress Catalog Card Number: 2017941593
Printed in the U.S.A.

CONTENTS

INTRODUCTION

Catechists must hand on the teachings of Christ to those being catechized; they must prepare them for the sacraments instituted by Christ; they must orient them toward life lived according to the moral teaching of Christ; and they must lead them to pray with Christ. Catechists must make the words of Christ their own; "My teaching is not my own but it is from the one who sent me," and they confess with Saint Paul, "I handed on to you… what I also received." **NATIONAL DIRECTORY FOR CATECHESIS, PAGE 101**

Thank you for hearing and answering the call you received to serve your parish community by being a volunteer catechist. You are fulfilling an important ministry in the Church by participating in spreading the Good News and handing on the treasures of the Catholic Faith.

The work you have agreed to do can indeed be a little scary—particularly if you don't have a lot of teaching experience. This little book won't calm all your fears or turn you instantly into a "Catechist of the Year," but we hope it will provide you with some inspiration and practical help—some "on the fly" formation for this important ministry.

The first three chapters of this book focus on you—who you are as a catechist, what kind of spirit you can have, and how you can learn more about the faith you share. The next three chapters focus on those to whom you minister—your students. These chapters help you see just who they are, how to keep them actively engaged in learning, and some good habits you can develop that will help your students. And there is a "quick-reference" glossary, too.

This guide is part of your personal catechetical tool kit, but it certainly should not be the only tool. We recommend that you treat yourself to four other tools to put into use in making you a better and more confident catechist:

1. **A Bible**: Make sure that you have an everyday Bible—not a fancy one with gold-edged pages. Get a Catholic Bible (Old and New Testament both) that you can write in, fold over pages, and mark with tabs and "stickies." This is a must.

2. The **Catechism of the Catholic Church** (CCC): It is important to have a copy of the official *Catechism*. Reading and studying the *Catechism* can help you grow in your understanding and appreciation of your Catholic faith, and it will help you stay focused on your task.

3. The **General Directory for Catechesis** (GDC): This book provides the attitudes and marching orders that parallel the content of the faith you find in the *Catechism*. It is not an easy book, but it is a very important one.

4. The **National Directory for Catechesis** (NDC): This book guides the Church in the United States in its catechetical ministry.

As far as this little book is concerned, there is no need to read it all at once. Keep it handy, and use it any way you see fit. We hope it helps you find joy and satisfaction in your important ministry.

1

ON *a* MISSION

Next to home and family, the witness of the catechist may be pivotal in every phase of the catechetical process. Under the guidance of the Holy Spirit, catechists powerfully influence those being catechized by their faithful proclamation of the Gospel of Jesus Christ and the transparent example of their Christian lives. For catechesis to be effective, catechists must be fully committed to Jesus Christ. They must firmly believe in his Gospel and its power to transform lives. **NATIONAL DIRECTORY FOR CATECHESIS, PAGE 101**

Catechists are called to a ministry—a vocation. Catechists are called to proclaim the message of the gospel. Over and over in the gospel, Jesus calls people and sets them on a mission. His last words to his disciples were couched in missionary language: "Go therefore and make disciples of all nations, baptizing them in the name of the Father and of the Son and of the Holy Spirit, and teaching them to obey everything that I have commanded you. And remember, I am with you always, to the end of the age" (Matthew 28:19–20).

Every Catholic parish has as one of its primary activities the duty to catechize its members. The word catechize literally means "to echo." It is easy to take that too literally and limit it to repeating prayers or teachings over and over. But in reality the whole life of the parish should echo

3

to all its members and to the whole community the gospel of Jesus and the richness of the Catholic tradition.

A Mission to Teach

The volunteer catechist is called by God and by the parish to teach. The gift of teaching is part of the ministry of the word. The catechist is appointed to share the knowledge of the faith as directed by the Church. In the epistles of Saint Paul—especially Romans and Corinthians—the gift of teaching gets special consideration. Teachers help to build up the body of Christ. Jesus was often referred to as rabbi, that is, "teacher."

It is true that a catechist teaches by word—using instructional materials, handing on the stories Jesus told and the events of his life, preparing young and old for initiation and the reception of the sacraments.

Yet part of the teaching mission is to teach by your living witness. Those you teach will not only be listening to you, they will also be watching you. Your actions and your attitudes are also part of your catechetical message.

Catechesis and Evangelization

"Go into the whole world and proclaim the gospel to every creature" (Mark 16:15). Christ has called all his followers to announce the Good News and to hand on his message. The picture of an evangelist as someone screaming a message at a television camera can give a person pause. Evangelization, however, takes place whenever faithful people profess, live, pray, and celebrate their faith. Evangelization is the lifelong partner of catechesis.

Pope John Paul II called for a "new" evangelization to the world so that in this new and information-packed age the good news of the kingdom can break through and call all to conversion in Christ. The process of evangelization includes "proclaiming Christ, preaching Christ, bearing witness to Christ, teaching Christ and celebrating Christ's sacraments" (NDC, page 49).

As part of this new evangelization, dioceses and parishes have been called to pursue some very important objectives. You may be experiencing some of them in your parish right now:

1. To foster personal conversion to Christ and greater participation in the life of the Mystical Body;

2. To encourage greater knowledge of sacred Scripture and the sacred Tradition of the Church;

3. To focus an effort on conversion and parish renewal by implementing the Rite of Christian Initiation of Adults (RCIA);

4. To continue liturgical renewal—especially for the celebration of Sunday Mass;

5. To make clear the evangelical and social justice dimension of the Sunday Eucharist;

6. To call for a renewal of daily prayer—the Liturgy of the Hours, the Rosary, and adoration of the Blessed Sacrament;

7. To make sure that all Catholic institutions—especially the parish— are welcoming and open to all.

The mission of catechesis is part of evangelization—especially in the RCIA. But catechesis is much more than that. Every Catholic participates in the process of catechesis. With the grace of God, catechesis develops that faith that was a response to hearing the good news. Catechesis nourishes Christian life. Catechesis constantly uncovers the mystery of Jesus Christ to encourage discipleship.

> *To put it more precisely: within the whole process of*
> *evangelization, the aim of catechesis is to be the teaching*

Part of a Great Tradition

Sometimes when you think about your ministry, you may find it hard to look beyond the runny noses, the cramped quarters your class occupies, the juggling of textbooks and art supplies. It can be quite difficult to get beyond all the details of preparing youngsters for First Holy Communion or confirmation. The drilling of the Ten Commandments or the corporal works of mercy may not seem all that important at the time.

Nonetheless, you are part of a great tradition and are fulfilling the mission that was shared by many of the great saints of the Church. Paul the Apostle, the patriarchs of the Church, Augustine and his mother Monica, Francis and Clare of Assisi, Thomas Aquinas, Francis de Sales, Elizabeth Ann Seton, John Neumann, Katharine Drexel, and hundreds more have helped people see and understand the mysteries of the gospel.

The United States has had a long and exciting tradition of fulfilling the catechetical mission. The immigrant Church in the nineteenth century understood that it had to keep the Catholic faith alive in sometimes very hostile places. The Councils of Baltimore worked to provide standards for that instruction. One of the products of those councils was the *Baltimore Catechism*—a compendium of what the Catholic Church believes and teaches. That Catechism was used for over one hundred years. In addition, Catholic schools were established in most parishes.

In the twentieth century, the popes and bishops promoted the Confraternity of Christian Doctrine (CCD) and mandated that every parish be involved in the catechesis of children and their preparation for first sacraments. The Confraternity trained lay people to teach the catechism to any and all who could not attend Catholic schools. Organizations like the Catholic Youth Organization (CYO) provided learning opportunities for adolescents and young people.

The Second Vatican Council spurred a renewal of catechesis. Interest in the Catholic faith grew. As economic times made it harder to support Catholic schools, parish catechesis expanded and grew—still referred to in many places as CCD. New textbooks were published. Dioceses began master catechist programs, national organizations were formed, and magazines were published. Today, over 500,000 men and women serve as parish catechists in this country. Each of them is dedicated to seeing that from the cradle to the grave the followers of Jesus can grow in their faith and be active members of Christ's Church.

That is just a taste of the great tradition to which you belong. Catechists and their mission often go unheralded. There is, however, a day set aside to celebrate the mission of Catechesis—Catechetical Sunday in September. In many parishes, that day marks the beginning of the year's catechetical program. Often the day includes a commissioning of parish catechists. This day is a day to celebrate the great tradition of catechesis and to show support for the men and women—just like you—who are on that mission.

A Word about the Story

Elie Wiesel, the Nobel Peace Prize winning author, wrote in the epigraph to his novel *Gates of the Forest* that God created people because God loves stories. Jesus used stories to proclaim God's kingdom. Paul and the Apostles spread the good news by sharing the stories of salvation and redemption.

As a catechist, you are also a storyteller. People of all ages learn from stories. You will be telling the greatest story ever. You will be telling stories about the lives of the saints. You will be sharing stories from the history of the Church. You will be using stories from daily life to show

God's grace active in the world or to show just how much God's grace is needed in the world.

Never forget the power of the story in your ministry. At the same time, never equate the word "story" with "fiction." Everyone understands that some stories are true stories and some stories are made up. If the greatest Teacher could use stories—true ones and crafted ones—then the art of the story should be in every catechist's tool kit.

Summary

You have been called to a very important mission in the Church. You are charged with faithfully handing on the good news of God's kingdom and helping people follow Jesus Christ. In that, you are fulfilling part of your baptismal covenant.

A Plan

1 Begin a catechetical library. The four books mentioned in the introduction to this little book are a must and will form the core of your library.

2 Conduct a little personal research on the history of the catechetical mission. Here are a few good websites to explore: The United States Conference of Catholic Bishops, usccb.org; The National Conference for Catechetical Leadership, nccl.org; The National Catholic Educational Association's Department of Parish Catechetical Directors, ncea.org.

3 Subscribe to your diocesan newspaper to stay abreast of all the events planned for catechists and for articles of interest for you and for the class you teach.

4 Write your own catechist covenant. In your own words, write a brief statement of your mission and how you, by God's grace, hope to fulfill that mission.

Prayerful Reflection

Read Luke 10:21–24. Spend some moments reflecting on what these words of Jesus say to you as a volunteer parish catechist. Write out your reflection.

2

DEVELOPING *a* CATECHETICAL SPIRIT

Catechesis, as communication of divine Revelation, is radically inspired by the pedagogy of God, as displayed in Christ and in the Church. It conveys God's loving plan of salvation in the person of Jesus Christ. It emphasizes God's initiative in this plan, his attentive disclosure of it, and his respect for individual liberty....It keeps Christ, the incarnate Word of God, ever at its center in order to bring humanity to God and God to humanity. It constantly draws inspiration from the Holy Spirit, who unfolds the mystery of Christ in the Church. **NATIONAL DIRECTORY FOR CATECHESIS, PAGE 94**

As a catechist, a lot of what you do is all wrapped up in preparing lessons, reading through lesson plans, hunting down DVDs, flitting around online to find reproducible art and activities, and preparing good questions. Once you get into your classroom you can get all involved in the clock, newsprint, scissors and glue, banners and quizzes, and the like. But what you bring to your catechetical mission is much more important than any of those things.

If you are to take your mission seriously, you need to have a catechetical spirituality. What that means at its root is that you believe the axiom that no one can give what he or she does not have. The task you have is to proclaim Christ's message, to develop the community of faith, to help people worship and pray, and to motivate them to serve others. More than anything else, you need to have a catechetical spirit. And so one element of your vocation as a catechist is the development of your faith and your spirituality.

This spirituality has several characteristics and not a few attitudes. Take a look at the characteristics first. Then you can review some of the attitudes. Remember that by your baptism, you have answered a universal call to holiness. And so, if you think some of these characteristics and attitudes smack of holiness, you are absolutely correct. But it is equally important to remember that holiness happens over time and it happens with God's grace. You are not flexing your own sanctity muscles. You are learning to respond to God's grace.

Characteristics

While there may be many characteristics of a catechetical spirit, here are a few for you to think about.

1. *You are called.* You are not sharing the faith because you think there is nobody better to do it. You are answering a call from Christ and the Church. You are honored and humbled by that call.

2. *You are willing to witness.* You are committed to Jesus Christ and his Church and you want to share that commitment. The Good News of salvation has made a difference to you, and you want it to make a difference in the lives of others.

3. *You represent the Church.* You are not working for yourself. You are fulfilling a need the People of God have for renewal and growth in the Holy Spirit. As a catechist you are loyal and faithful.

4. *You are a witness to community.* You know that the faith is not about "me and God." You know that the Church is a community of believers who worship together, who seek reconciliation, who strive for holiness together.

5. *You are willing to serve.* Your spirit is characterized by service. The ministry you perform is not about you. It is about those you teach.

6. *You are willing to learn.* Your spirituality is characterized by a great willingness to admit that you have a lot to learn and to go about learning.

Catechetical Attitudes

Jesus did not choose perfect people to spread the good news of God's kingdom. You were called to be a catechist because you are a participating member of your parish who has shown the spirit and the ability to share your faith with others. At the same time, because you have answered the call, you no doubt will wonder about your ability or your spirit. First of all, the spirituality of the catechist is open to God's action and grace in his or her life.

Catechists can also do an attitude check to see how they are growing in those Catholic attitudes that will help them grow in faith, share the faith, and witness to the faith. The questions can help you assess your catechetical spirit and can lead you to areas in your ministry that can help you be more open to the grace you need to be a better and better catechist.

1. *Is my catechetical spirit grounded in the life of the Trinity?* Do I address my prayers to the Father—the Lord and Creator of all? Do I understand and believe that Jesus Christ, his only Son, became truly human and yet remained truly God? Do I realize that the Holy Spirit draws all humanity to Christ and through Christ into communion with the Trinity?

2. ***Does the word of God form and inform my spirit?*** Do I read the Bible often? Would I consider myself to be a "person of the gospel?" Am I anxious to learn more about Scripture? Do I ever read the Sunday readings beforehand, and do I listen attentively to them at Mass? Do I try to apply the words of the gospel to my life?

3. ***Am I a grateful person?*** Do I realize that all I have and am is a gift from God? Am I gracious with others as well—showing appreciation and gratitude?

4. ***Am I a sacramental person?*** Do I realize that God communicates through signs and symbols that I can see and hear and taste? Do I understand the importance of the sacraments for the life of the Church?

5. ***Am I a Eucharistic person?*** Do I attend Mass regularly—even at times other than Sunday? Do I actively participate in the Mass? Do I receive Holy Communion with devotion and with a thankful spirit?

6. ***Am I aware that I belong to a community of faith?*** Do I realize that being a Catholic means an initiation into the communion of saints? Do I also realize that the community will help form me in my Catholic faith?

7. ***Am I faithful to God and to the Church?*** Do I understand and believe what the Church believes and teaches? Do I strive to be loyal and faithful to the Church? Do I realize that I do not always have complete understanding of Church teaching, and so strive to learn more?

8. ***Am I generous, open, and welcoming?*** Do I know that the way I live my life can attract others to Christ and to his Church? Do I have a welcoming spirit in my dealings with others? Do I understand the important role the Rite of Christian Initiation plays in the life of my parish and of the whole Church?

9. ***Am I a person of prayer?*** Is prayer important to me? Do I set aside what time I can to spend in prayer? Do I nourish my prayer with spiritual reading, quiet time, and participation in Catholic devotions such as the Rosary or other more formal prayers?

10. ***Do I both seek and offer forgiveness?*** Am I willing to forgive those who have hurt me or do I carry grudges? Do I seek forgiveness when I have hurt others? Is participation in the sacrament of penance an important part of my spiritual life?

11. ***Do I strive to be a peaceful and just person?*** Do I understand and communicate the social teachings of the Church? Do I seek to understand the Catholic teaching about the sacredness of life in all its aspects?

12. ***Do I see my own home and family as the Church?*** Do we strive to pray together as a family, attend Sunday Mass together, share quality time together, and live the gospel in our everyday lives?

13. ***Am I a joyful person?*** Do I give witness to the joy of belonging to the People of God? Do I show that I understand that real joy comes from knowing, loving, and serving God?

All this may sound a little like an "examination of conscience." In fact, however, the posing of all these questions—coupled with your honest answers—provides some indication of what kind of person a catechist strives to be.

Your Call to Holiness

The National Directory puts the spiritual growth of the catechist in the context of the universal call to holiness.

> *Like all the faithful, catechists are called to holiness. Because*
> *of their ministry and mission, however, the call to holiness has*

a particular urgency. The spiritual life of a catechist should be characterized by:

- *A love of God—Father, Son, and Holy Spirit—and of Christ's Church, our Holy Father, and God's holy people*

- *A coherence and authenticity of life that is characterized by their faithful practice of the faith in a spirit of faith, charity, hope, courage, and joy*

- *Personal prayer and dedication to the evangelizing mission of the Church*

- *A missionary zeal by which they are fully convinced of the truth of the Catholic faith and enthusiastically proclaim it*

- *Active participation in their local parish community, especially by attendance at Sunday Eucharist*

- *A devotion to Mary, the first disciple and the model of catechists, and to the Most Holy Eucharist, the source and nourishment for catechists*

NATIONAL DIRECTORY FOR CATECHESIS, PAGE 229

Your Spiritual Growth

As a catechist, your spiritual growth is an important part of the ministry. You realize that you are very human—with strengths and weaknesses, virtues and vices. But you also are well aware that you are not a catechist to put forth your own private notions about God or religion or the Bible. You are a catechist in order to hand on God's living Word and the teaching and tradition of the Catholic Church.

What you do is very important—as is the care you put into your ministry. How you show your care will communicate much to your students about just how much Christ and his Church care for them. You want them to experience God's love and to share that love with others. You share that "love is patient; love is kind; love is not envious or boastful or arrogant or rude. It does not insist on its own way; it is not irritable or resentful; it does not rejoice in wrongdoing, but rejoices in the truth" (1 Corinthians 13:4–6).

If you can see that clearly, then you have a catechetical heart—you are graced with the Holy Spirit to keep the faith alive for yourself and for others.

Summary

Your positive response to the call to be a catechist says a lot about your heart and about your spirit. Use all the opportunities you can to grow in your catechetical spirituality.

A Plan

1 Set aside some personal prayer time each week.

2 If your teacher's manual has a catechist reflection, build that reflection into your preparation time.

3 Get into the Bible reading habit. Plan fifteen minutes a week of Scripture reading, or read over the Sunday readings in advance.

4 Set aside days to attend a weekday Mass—maybe to celebrate a saint's feast day or some family event.

5 Get a spiritual director or at least a catechetical partner to talk with about the spiritual challenges of your shared ministry.

Prayerful Reflection

Read Matthew 5:13–19. Think about how your own spiritual growth can help you be the salt of the earth and a light for the world. Write out a brief summary of your reflection.

____

____

3

KNOW YOUR FAITH

The sacred duty and the joy of each succeeding generation of Christian believers has been to hand on the deposit of faith that was first entrusted to the apostles by Christ himself. We have received this gift, the deposit of faith—we have not conceived it. It is the heritage of the whole Church. It is our privilege and our responsibility to preserve the memory of Christ's words and the words themselves and to teach future generations of believers to carry out all that Christ commanded his apostles.

NATIONAL DIRECTORY FOR CATECHESIS, PAGE 87

As a catechist, you are responsible to hand on the authentic Catholic faith. You do not hand on your own ideas about religion or the ideas found in weekly TV dramas or in popular novels. Your ministry, therefore, requires that you know your faith. It doesn't require that you be a seminary graduate or have an advanced degree in Scripture or theology. It does require that you become not simply a teacher, but a learner as well.

You have seen that sacred Scripture and sacred Tradition as outlined in the ***Catechism of the Catholic Church*** are the sources for instruction. The textbooks you have been given to use are important for authentic teaching as well. A committee of the bishops has reviewed those texts to make sure that they contain complete and authentic teaching. In addition, the teacher's manuals that support those textbooks often contain background material for the catechists. So, one way to make sure that you are handing on the faith is to use carefully and well the tools you are given.

A Personal Checklist

How do you know that you are teaching the truth of the Catholic faith? A simple checklist might help you analyze what you are doing and how you are doing it. If you regularly ask yourself the questions in the checklist, you will find yourself growing in your knowledge of the faith and your confidence that you are being faithful to your mission.

1. ***Does your teaching center on Jesus Christ?*** In your lessons, in your conversations with your students, in answering their questions, in the games you play, and the activities you share, Christ should be at the center of all. How often to you bring the ideas you are sharing back to Jesus? How comfortable are you in sharing your own faith in Christ?

2. ***Does your teaching of the gospel message introduce the Blessed Trinity to those you teach?*** Do you introduce each class with the Sign of the Cross? Do you anchor your own faith in the Blessed Trinity? How often are you aware of the role of the Trinity—Father, Son, and Holy Spirit—in the time you spend with your students?

3. ***Does your teaching tell about the good news of salvation?*** Are your students aware that God's own Son came to save all from sin and death? Do you make your students aware that they have been set free to know, love, and serve God in this world and to be happy with him in the next?

4. ***Does your teaching come from the Church and lead your students to the Church?*** Are your students aware that you are not teaching what you think, but what the Church believes and teaches? Do you try to instill in your students a love for the Church—the People of God?

5. *In your teaching do you show awareness that the Church has a long history and tradition?* Are your students aware of the importance of tradition? Do you use examples from the lives of the saints or from history to show how grounded in tradition the faith is?

6. *Do you speak the students' language, but do not water down the Catholic faith?* Do you know what is important to your students? Do you seek ways to communicate the faith in images and language the students understand? Do you try to make sure that you are still communicating the content of the faith?

7. *Is your teaching comprehensive?* Do you realize that not everything has the same importance? Are you aware that your students need to know the basics of sacred Scripture, the elements of the Creed, the mystery of the Church, baptism and the sacraments—especially the Eucharist, love of God and love of neighbor, and prayer?

8. *Does your teaching stress human dignity?* Do you teach about the meaning of life? Do you demonstrate the meaning of the Beatitudes? Do you teach about hope?

9. *Do you teach the common language of the faith?* Does your teaching help your students understand how Catholics talk about their faith? Do you use the words and definitions that are part of that conversation?

Four Big Categories

The *Catechism of the Catholic Church* is divided into four major sections. Those sections show how the content of the Catholic faith is organized. When a catechist answers the call to teach, he or she understands that the catechetical message needs to include all four to be truly complete.

The first section of the *Catechism* covers the *Profession of Faith*. It contains the teaching about the Blessed Trinity, Creation, Grace, and the life, death, and resurrection of Jesus, the communion of saints, and the rest. It teaches, too, about the role that Mary plays in the life of the Church and the lives of Christians.

The second section is about *Celebrating the Christian Mystery*. It demonstrates how important it is for members of the Church to understand and to participate in the sacraments. It shows how baptism, confirmation, and Eucharist are sacraments of initiation, how penance and anointing are sacraments of healing, and how holy orders and matrimony are sacraments in service of the community. It also helps believers to understand the central place of the sacrifice of the Mass—the great celebration of thanksgiving and communion.

The third section focuses on *Life in Christ*. In this section you will find the moral teachings of the Church. It shows how grace helps people live good and virtuous lives. It shows that Catholics don't only "talk the talk." They also "walk the walk"—following in the footsteps of Jesus Christ.

The final section is on *Prayer*. Catholics do indeed pray. They pray together and they pray alone. In prayer and reflection, they discover and come to understand the Christian mysteries. They also understand that the *Lord's Prayer* is of particular importance for their lives.

A Relationship

As a catechist you are witnessing to the Catholic faith. You are handing on the basic teachings of the Church. Most of all, you are showing that faith is at its heart a relationship.

God offered a covenant of friendship to people. "You are my people, and I am your God!" Still, relationships involve struggles. And relationships with God and with the Church are no exception. You may even have your own struggles with your faith. But the part of knowing your faith is trusting in the relationship and relying on one of the great gifts God has given—the Holy Spirit. As a teacher, you need in a special way the gifts that the Holy Spirit gives:

1. *Wisdom*—the gift of seeing that there is more to life than meets the eye: Wisdom helps you realize that you are not the final authority.

2. *Understanding*—the gift of seeing how things fit together: Understanding helps make sense out of life.

3. *Counsel*—the gift of knowing right from wrong: Counsel helps you know what is true, beautiful, and right in life.

4. *Knowledge*—the gift of looking for the truth and recognizing it when you have found it: Knowledge never substitutes opinion for the facts or current fashion for eternal truth.

5. *Fortitude*—the gift of facing difficulties: Fortitude is a catechist's great need when it is hard to go into the classroom and witness to what is right.

6. *Piety*—the gift of right priorities: Piety is the ability to give reverence and worship to God and the ability not to put created things in first position in one's life.

7. *Fear of the Lord*—the gift of being aware of God's presence and amazed at the gift of life. Fear of the Lord is not horror or terror. Rather it does not take God for granted, and it sees his footprints everywhere.

A Word about Doubt

You know how important it is to know your faith if you are called to teach it. But does that mean you have to be perfectly free of any doubt? Doubt is part of the process. If faith meant certitude, why would it be called faith? Your personal doubts, however, are challenged by the faithfulness of the community. You do not believe all on your own; you have the Church to fall back on. As a catechist, one of the worst things you can do is visit your doubts on those you teach. Here are a couple of habits you can develop to face your doubts and bring them to the community.

1. *Be honest about your doubts.* It doesn't help to pretend that you have no doubts.

2. *Be open to having your doubts looked at by wiser members of the Church—a priest or spiritual director.* Some people are more in love with their doubts than they are with their faith. They want to hang on to the doubt no matter what.

3. *Be patient with yourself.* You can't know or understand everything about your faith. Learning to believe is the task of a lifetime. You may just have to set aside your doubts and pray for the help of the Holy Spirit.

4. *Be sensitive to the faith of others.* Some people are better at sharing doubt than they are at sharing faith. Your own personal doubts and misgivings should be shared at appropriate times with people whose wisdom you trust. Doubt should never be sown like seeds of discontent.

5. *Pray to overcome doubt.* Share often the prayer of the father of the possessed boy in Mark's gospel. "I do believe. Help my lack of trust!" (Mark 9:24).

Summary

Remember that knowing the faith is important for all Catholics. It is all the more important for those who answer the call to the catechetical ministry. Remember, too, that you always have lots to learn.

A Plan

1 Keep a diary to track your discoveries about your faith. You might divide your diary into five categories: Sacred Scripture, Profession of Faith, Celebrating the Christian Mysteries, Life in Christ, and Prayer.

2 Find out where you can get some catechist formation.

3 Participate in adult classes in your parish.

4 Have a reading plan. Put together a list of three or four religious books you will read during the coming year. Be sure to take notes on your reading.

5 Use the lesson background material in your teacher's manual.

Prayerful Reflection

Pray the whole of Psalm 27. This psalm is loaded with attitudes that can help you as a catechist. When you have read the psalm, reflect on its sentiments for a few moments. Then summarize your reactions.

4

KNOW YOUR STUDENTS

Just as Christ instructed his followers according to their capacity to understand his message, the Church also must take serious account of the circumstances and cultures in which the faithful live in order to present the meaning of the Gospel to them in understandable ways. There is one saving word—Jesus Christ—but that word can be spoken in many different ways. The "adaptation and preaching of the revealed Word must ever be the law of all evangelism." **NATIONAL DIRECTORY FOR CATECHESIS, PAGE 186**

Of course it is important for a catechist to know the Faith, but why is it so important to know the students? For one thing, Saint Thomas Aquinas pointed out "whatever is learned is learned after the manner of the learner." Put another way, if you understand the students you teach, you will better be able to reach them. And a teacher has no sadder lament than "I just can't reach those kids!"

Take a few minutes to think about how you learn best. Do you like to read the instructions that come with a new cell phone or a piece of furniture that has "some assembly required"? Do you dive right into a project and bumble through by trial and error? Do you call the help line at the first sign of computer trouble? Or do you click around until something happens? Do you remember telephone numbers when you hear them, or do you have to write them down at once or they are gone forever?

The answers you have to those questions say something about you as a learner. As a catechist, you need to know that each student you teach has a style of learning. The better you feed those learning styles, the better you will reach the students with the good news of Jesus Christ and the teachings of his Church.

"Wait a minute," you might say, "I only have these students for about an hour a week—fewer than twenty-five hours a year. How in heaven's name can I discover each of their learning styles? How can I teach to meet all those styles?"

Well, unless you are a whiz at social sciences, you probably can't. What you can do is make an effort to meet some of the basic styles. It also helps if you realize some basic characteristics of the age group you teach. Let's begin with a quick tour of the age groups followed by a summary of some learning styles. Remember for a moment what kind of teacher Jesus was. Jesus grounded his teaching in the language and life of the people he was teaching. He used stories of fishermen, farmers, and vineyard workers. He told simple stories. Jesus also taught with signs— healing, turning water into wine, raising from the dead, helping a blind man see, or making a leper clean. By his own life, Jesus taught lessons on prayer, courage, doing what is right, even on death for others. Jesus understood the way God teaches and the way people learn.

The Young Child (Preschool through Grade 3)

The young child is spontaneous and quite energetic. Young children see themselves at the center of everything. They have a great sense of wonder, they love ritual, and (of course) they need to feel safe and cared for. They have very short attention spans, however. They also tend to be quite active—even jittery. That is because their young minds are absorbing information all the time.

Their senses are attuned to all sorts of stimuli—noise, smell, color, music, taste, and the like. They want approval, and they will imitate the kindness, respect, and language of those around them. They are wide open to learning about God, and they easily see God's footprints in the world around them.

Younger children learn by doing, by repeating ideas and actions. Their religious development depends on simple and very concrete experiences. They are capable of handling quite a bit if the lessons are given with lots of illustrations, are couched in simple language, and are repeated frequently. The young religious learner loves to pray and loves the sights and sounds of the liturgy.

The Older Child (Grades 4 to 6)

Older children love heroes and role models. Independence and curiosity are in conflict in them. They ask questions till the air is filled with the sounds of "Who? What? Why? How? How much? Can I?"

This age group likes facts and specific activities such as measuring, compiling, counting, and the like. They are beginning to see that life is governed by rules, and they can easily become junior lawyers whose harshest judgment is "That's not fair!" They are gaining a sense of history as well as cause and effect. They are also beginning to see the consequences of their actions. They are becoming comfortable with group activities.

The Adolescent

The range of adolescence is quite a big one. The lower end of adolescence is filled with growing, testing, and searching. The young adolescent is no longer just a child, but he or she is not quite ready to be an adult. The changes of puberty affect the learning of the young adolescent. They are looking for personal identity, and they rely on the approval of their peers.

At the upper ranges of adolescence, the future is looming with its challenges and its perils. The alienation that the older adolescent feels can drive toward the positive conclusions of self-motivation and life choices, or it can lead to depression and anger. At all stages of adolescence, the teenagers need respect and acceptance. They are susceptible to challenge and good example. They also are looking for moral direction and solid roots. They also crave the spiritual and transcendent.

The Adult

Children and adolescents need direction in their learning. The "curriculum" comes from outside. Adults learn because they need to or really want to. More and more colleges, for example, tailor their catalogues and degree requirements to fit changing needs on the part of their students. Some college students are stuck in adolescence and others are taking to learning like need-driven adults.

As a person matures, the needs change. In midlife, there may be need to alter directions at work, in the family, in the faith. In older years, there is the need to reflect, to look back, to learn what seems to have been missing, or to face the frailty of old age. Most of all, adults need to see the importance and benefit of what they are invited to learn.

Helping Faith Grow

Obviously, the descriptions of each of these groups of learners are just quick highlights. They do show you, however, how important it is for a catechist to be aware of these differences. Catechesis has as one of its tasks the nurturing of faith. So, understanding that faith does not happen all at once is an important part of knowing the learner.

The product of all catechetical efforts is an adult believer of mature faith. A person of mature faith has an attitude of conversion to the Lord, has made a decision to live the gift of faith within the Catholic Church, and is willing to be a Christian disciple in the world. The adult believer is knowledgeable and informed. He or she is not swayed by emotions or changes in others. A mature believer's faith is personal and does not depend on the actions or inactions of others. A person of mature faith is humble—knowing that he or she does not have all the answers. He or she relies on the authentic teaching of the Church.

That is why it is also important to know a little bit about learning styles. Children and adults will share these styles. Almost everyone has a predominant learning style. It is not feasible in such a short guide (as practical as it might be) to go into great length about learning styles. But it can be helpful for you to look at a capsule of a few of the styles. Some books on learning styles stick to more physical aspects of learning. Are you primarily an aural learner—do you learn by listening? Are you primarily a visual learner—do you learn by seeing? For religious instruction, it might be helpful to take another tack and look at other learning factors.

Imagination

Some learners are imaginative learners. They are interested in the context of learning. They are the children who ask, "Why do we need to know this?" or "Why is this important?" They crave interpersonal relationships and feel a strong need to belong. They like to talk and get their motivation from feelings rather than ideas. Imaginative learners need to be drawn into a lesson. This style of learner can also be disruptive and can monopolize discussion. Their needs for emotional stimulus and approval can make them quite susceptible to peer pressure.

Analysis

Some learners (even quite young ones) can be quite analytical. They want facts. They like an orderly and quiet learning environment. They are usually motivated by the content itself. These are the students teachers love because they seem to just love logic and learning. They can be quite competitive and can consider themselves quite smart, even though they may be no more or less so than other-style learners. The downside of the analytical learner is the "smarty-pants" syndrome. They have a strong need to be right, and may not be willing to see more than one side of an issue.

Common Sense

Some people just learn better by doing. Such learners are not always at ease in a traditional classroom. They look for action as a way to learn.

They tend to be practical with little patience for speculation. They abide planning as long as it leads to action. They are can-do folks who jump right into technical or mechanical problems. They prefer to work alone, and they love demonstrations rather than lectures. In the catechetical setting, these learners plan and put on skits or prayer services or parties. They might like building a model of Solomon's Temple better than memorizing answers for a quiz. Their downside is their very task orientation. They can be harsh and disconnected and their action orientation can turn to cynicism. They are not always good at interpersonal relationships.

Creativity

Some learners seem dynamic. They have big ideas. They tend to be creative or innovative and they take risks. Often these learners are artistic. Creative learners tend to be leaders and good communicators. Such learners need options and like a flexible learning environment. They enjoy people but often work alone. They are seldom satisfied with the status quo and need a variety of approaches if they are to stay engaged. Creative learners are quick to teach others what they have learned. They are also quick to dramatize stories with great production value. Creative learners are sometimes excitable and even a bit unruly. They don't always finish what they start. Their big ideas can make them sound arrogant at times.

Summary

Knowing all you can about the students you teach will make you a better catechist. And because most teachers teach in the same way they learn best, it is important for you to learn your own style.

A Plan

1 Do some online searching about learning styles.

2 Keep a log. Jot down your observations on what activities worked best in your class and how various students reacted to those exercises.

3 Cultivate variety. You might not reach all learning styles with every lesson, but if you vary your approach, you will do so quite often.

4 Develop alternate approaches to lessons. Learn flexibility and how to respond to the reactions you get from the class.

5 Get an observer. Ask someone you trust to watch you in action. Get that person to give you some honest feedback on how well you know your students.

Prayerful Reflection

Read Luke 24:13–32. After the reading think about what you have read. Then write how Jesus adapted his lesson to his students in that reading.

____

____

5

KEEP LEARNING ACTIVE

Catechesis links human experience to the revealed word of God, helping people ascribe Christian meaning to their own existence. It enables people to explore, interpret, and judge their basic experiences in light of the Gospel. Catechesis helps them relate the Christian message to the most profound questions in life; the existence of God, the destiny of the human person, the origin and end of history, the truth about good and evil, the meaning of suffering and death, and so forth. By recalling God's salvific action in human history, catechesis helps people to recognize their need for conversion and leads them to conversion in Christ.

NATIONAL DIRECTORY FOR CATECHESIS, PAGE 98

If you have ever been to a talk or a class in a huge lecture hall, you may have had the experience of listening to someone give a well-crafted presentation of some topic to the group. Everyone dutifully would take notes. When the presentation was over, the person left the room. If the talk was very good, this may have been a fairly satisfying experience, but not an ideal situation for catechesis.

As a catechist, your mission is much more than telling your students about the wonders of the Catholic faith, the holy Bible, the liturgy of the

Church, the steps in following Jesus, or Christian prayer. Your task is to keep them actively engaged in the process. The songs you sing together, the pictures you draw, the skits you perform, the ritual actions you share, the questions and answers, the quizzes, and the memorization—all those little elements keep the learning active.

Methodology

You know the power of God's word. As the Prophet Isaiah said about the word of God, "For as the rain and the snow come down from heaven, and do not return there until they have watered the earth, making it bring forth and sprout, giving seed to the sower and bread to the eater, so shall my word be that goes out from my mouth; it shall not return to me empty, but it shall accomplish that which I purpose, and succeed in the thing for which I sent it" (Isaiah 55:10–11).

God's own methodology included sending the Word made Flesh—his only Son—to make known the mysteries of his divine plan. The life and teaching of Jesus were active and on the move. The life, death, resurrection, and glorious ascension of Jesus Christ were teaching moments that demanded a response. When the Apostles at Pentecost—filled with the Holy Spirit—gave out the good news, the response of their "students" was "What shall we do?" From the very earliest days in the life of the Church, that catechesis has continued.

Any and all methods you employ as a catechist are aimed not at the knowledge, but at the response of faith on the part of the learner. To do that, the learner needs to be actively engaged in the process. And so, whatever methods you use when you are in the classroom, you want to:

- Emphasize God's call and the learner's free response;

- Accept that you can't teach everything at once and need to adapt what you are teaching to the level of your student;

- Always show the centrality of Jesus Christ;

- Demonstrate and give value to the Christian community;

- Enter a relationship with your students and
give them a chance for dialogue;

- Draw on signs, symbols, and exercises that link words
with deeds and learning with experience;

- Draw on the power of the truth of what you teach and
trust in the actions and grace of the Holy Spirit.

The Church has never relied on just one method to share the good news. And all human methods have been used. For a more detailed discussion of the following points, you might read the NDC, pages 87-107.

1. *Human Experience:* Jesus used human experience to connect with his audiences. Human experiences provide the signs that lead a person, by the grace of the Holy Spirit, to an understanding of the truths of the faith. One of the best ways to keep learning active is to relate what you are teaching with the real experiences of your students. Be careful, however, not to use your experiences as a substitute for your students' experiences. You are teaching them to see God's love and grace in their lives—not yours.

2. *Discipleship:* Help your students learn to follow Jesus. As those of us who have chosen to be disciples grow and mature, the desire to follow brings out the truths of the faith. Children, who may not be able to understand and articulate all the truths of the faith, have a unique ability to celebrate the most profound truths of the faith. Children are capable of being formed as disciples from an early age.

3. *The Christian Community:* The life of the parish is loaded with teachable moments. The worship, service, fellowship, and strivings of the community are excellent examples of catechesis in action. It is most import-

ant to ground your own teaching in the life of the community.

4. _The Christian Family:_ Children ordinarily have their first catechetical experiences within their Christian home. Because it is the "church of the home," the family is an ideal place for sharing and receiving the word of God. In your teaching be aware of the rule of the home and the family, and make sure to link what you do to the home. In addition, be sure to send home with the children discussions and activities that can help the family share God's love.

5. _Your Witness:_ You are the best tool for keeping learning active. Next to the home and family, your witness may be pivotal in all phases of the process. Of course, you need to firmly believe in the gospel and its power to transform lives.

6. _Memorization:_ One of the keys to active learning is the method of learning "by heart." Although the faith can never be reduced to formulas, committing certain things to memory can fix them in a student's mind and bring them to the fore when they are needed. Every Catholic should know certain prayers by heart. In addition, it is helpful to know certain passages from the Bible by heart as well. It is also important to know the Creed, the parts of the Mass, the holy days, and the mysteries of the Rosary. Those formulas that deal with the moral life of Christians should also be memorized—the commandments, the Beatitudes, the gifts of the Holy Spirit, the virtues, and the precepts of the Church. Every Catholic should also know a simple examination of conscience by heart.

7. _Other Methods:_ There are many ways to impart the faith. Most published catechetical programs use a great variety of methods that will keep your students active and engaged. One of the most important things you can do to grow as a catechist is to become comfortable with those methods and use as many of them as you can. Games, activities, crafts, music, and gestures—all of these will help keep learning active for the students you teach. All of these methods have one goal—to proclaim God's love and God's kingdom.

A Word about Arts and Crafts

Arts and crafts are important in the catechesis of children (and one could argue for their use with older learners as well). Young people express and develop creativity in many ways. Painting, cutting and pasting, drawing and coloring—all these creative activities allow for self-expression and facilitate sharing.

Older youngsters will work well independently. They are comfortable with their abilities. Younger children will need more help. Be sure to always let your students know the reason for art or craft activities. The activities should be natural, spontaneous, free, and enjoyable.

It is important to keep projects simple. The use of arts and crafts is not an end in itself. Look for cooperative art projects—such as murals, banners, or posters—to foster community and sharing. Don't be afraid to participate yourself. Don't use craft activities as a chance to take a nap or read the newspaper. Your participation will show the importance of these catechetical activities.

There are two arts and crafts "sins." The first is to reduce all of your catechetical time to drawing or pasting. The second is not to use artwork at all. Artwork is important for all the disciplines the children learn at school. It should be just as important for their catechetical work.

A variety of arts and crafts projects will help you reach the different learning styles of the students you teach.

The Media

Electronic media are everywhere today. Everyone (who is not in a Rip Van Winkle sleep) is exposed to fast moving images, music, color, and sound effects in live action or animation.

The students you teach will also find a kind of formation in the media they consume. It is an important part of keeping learning active for you to use the visual and audio media in your class. That accomplishes two things. It engages the students, but it also makes the students more literate about what they watch and listen to. There are a couple of very good rules to follow as far as using media is concerned:

- Always preview what you are going to show. That way you will never be embarrassed because of content that does not reflect your catechetical message;

- Never use a DVD or a video game as a "babysitter." Always talk about what you have seen and heard. You can have the students recall images, identify feelings and emotions raised, clarify the message, look for consequences in the actions, and so forth;

- Be sure to make a judgment about what you intend to use in class. No matter how highly recommended a bit of media is, make sure that you make your own judgment about it;

- Look for media with religious content. There are many films and songs that teach good moral lessons, but try also to use media that is overtly religious in content and tone.

As far as the media is concerned, it is good for you as a catechist to keep up on what games, movies, songs, and books are popular with the students you teach. Listen to your class to pick up on clues to what they are watching and listening to. Listen to the radio—you will hear the popular culture that is affecting the students you teach. If you have sampled what your students are consuming, you will better be able to show its relationship (or lack of relationship) to the good news of Jesus.

Summary

The time you take to learn more and more about keeping learning active is never wasted. Part of your formation as a catechist should be to become more and more comfortable with all the various ways of imparting the message.

A Plan

1 Prepare your lessons. The better prepared you are for the teaching you do, the more likely you are to include various methods that keep your students engaged and active. If you are unprepared, you will fall back on whatever is easiest at the moment.

2 Keep a log of things you do in class that keep the students active and engaged. The log will help you offer a variety of activities and exercises.

3 Swap experiences with other catechists. Sometimes the best source of teaching tips for active learning come from your peers in the catechetical ministry.

4 Subscribe to a catechetical magazine or newsletter (like *Catechist*).

Prayerful Reflection

Read Luke 19:11–26 and John 2:1–11. Reflect about how these two catechetical moments engaged the people that Jesus was teaching. How did they engage you? Write a summary of your reflection.

____

____

DEVELOP PRACTICAL HABITS

Called by the Holy Spirit, inspired by the dynamism of Christ's compelling mission, and sent by the Church, catechists make Christ and his Church known, loved, and followed by faithful disciples and by those who do not yet know him. They bring the word of God to adults, young people, and children....The heart of the catechist speaks the word of God to the heart of the one being catechized. Into their hearts, by the power of the Holy Spirit, the Father and the Son will come to make their dwelling.

NATIONAL DIRECTORY FOR CATECHESIS, PAGE 279

A good deal of this little guide has focused on you, on your spirit, and on your mission. The ministry of a good catechist is made up of those very important things, but it is also made up of routines and habits as well. A teacher gets the opportunity to develop habits over almost two hundred class days a year. You don't have that same luxury because most catechists meet with their classes twenty-five times a year. You may have to work a bit harder to develop some of those practical habits.

This chapter will give you some habits to think about and to develop. At the end of the chapter there is a note about some good procedures for dealing with and talking about the families of your students. First, take a look at some of the habits. They are organized into categories.

1. Environmental Habits

These habits have to do with the atmosphere and environment of your teaching place—classroom, home, or a spot on the gym floor.

- Maintain a very pleasant and clean environment. This habit is conducive to good discipline and productive work.

- Learn to make the best use of whatever space you have. Don't be haphazard. Keep the space organized.

- Add beauty, color, surprise, and other qualities to the environment. Religious pictures, posters, and banners make your class a pleasant place to be.

- Create a special place for prayer and get in the habit of beginning and ending every session with a prayer. This habit or routine is a lesson in itself.

2. Personal Habits

The teaching habits you develop will contribute to the productivity and success of your teaching. Some of these habits are pretty obvious, but unless you work on them, they will not come naturally and spontaneously.

- Always prepare your lesson. This is the most important personal habit you can develop. Everybody is too busy, but if you are unprepared, it will show. You will be giving a negative lesson on the importance of the Catholic faith.

- Arrive early for class. It is very difficult to conduct a smooth and effective class without the catechist being the first to arrive.

This habit goes hand in hand with the next personal habit.

- Know everyone's name and use it. It would be ideal if you would greet each of your students by name as they arrive for each session. In any event, use names frequently. Using nametags is a very helpful way to get this done, but if you are still using nametags in May, you did not work hard enough on mastering your student's names. Use a seating chart or any other device to make it easier to remember the names.

- Learn several methods for dividing the class into smaller groups for discussion. This kind of habit keeps things moving smoothly. If these techniques are not habitual, your class can get jumbled.

- Develop the habit of treating your students with respect. Don't be too familiar and don't be too removed. Be accepting and understanding, but be firm and honest. And, of course, develop the habit of awareness that you are teaching by actions as well as words.

3. Rules

A very good (and practical) catechetical habit is to develop rules for your class before the rules become necessary. Some clear rules and the habit of enforcing them will make your job easier and the learning atmosphere much better. You might even consider making a simple "learning covenant" with the class. You can help the students turn the elements of the covenant into habits as well. Here are some possible elements of such a covenant.

- There will be no putdowns in the class.

- Everyone will get a chance to participate, and everyone will make a point to participate.

- When the catechist calls for quiet, everyone will respond by the count of three.

- Everyone will pay attention.

- Everyone will treat one another with respect. (You get the idea.)

4. Discipline

Hand in hand with rules comes the habit of good discipline. This habit
starts with good preparation. If you spend the beginning of the class just
chatting with the class, discipline will be hard to maintain. If your class
sees that you have a plan and that you mean business, discipline will
become a habit for your students as well. When corrections are needed
(and they will be—even in a class filled with adults), be firm but not
angry—definitely not hostile. Even corrections should be made with
respect and honesty. A parallel habit is the ability to recognize when
corrections are needed. You are not running a boot camp. If your class
has a pleasant hum, you probably have good discipline.

5. Be yourself

One of the most important and practical habits you can have is to be
open and consistent. If you are, you will be at ease with your students
and they with you.

6. The Variety Habit

Provide a variety of experiences. This habit goes along with some of the
things you learned about keeping learning active. Unless you work at
this and make it habitual, you will find yourself falling back into teaching patterns that are comfortable for you but that may not be providing
good and profitable experiences for the students.

7. Organization

Not everybody gets an A in organization. There are several shows on television that feature attempts to get people's lives and "stuff" in order. One habit that will pay great dividends for you is keeping your materials and your resources in good order. Here are a couple of practical ideas that might help you with your organizational task.

- Keep all your lesson materials in one place. If you do not have a classroom that is for your use and your use alone, get a box with handles for everything you use in class on a regular basis—teacher's manual, Bible, newsprint, music player and disks, pencils, writing paper, duplicated materials.

- Keep and maintain an art box. Have all the basics in the box—crayons or markers, art paper, clay, glue, pens, and so forth. This will keep you from running out or finding yourself without the art supplies you need.

- Use lists. Because you do not teach every day, it will be difficult for you to keep everything in your head. Making lists will help you with preparation and with class.

- Keep a calendar. Every catechetical program runs on a schedule of classes. Make sure that you have that schedule in your calendar.

A Word about Privacy and Families

As a catechist, you relate not only to the students you teach but to their families as well. As you learned earlier, you play an important role in the lives of your students. They will no doubt be going home and quoting you—even using you as an authority. If you keep it clear in your mind that your task is information and not reformation, you will be well on your way to relating well to the families. There are some other good habits you can develop that will help you relate well with the children and with their families. Remember that we live in stressful times. Sometimes the most innocent actions on your part can take on meanings you never intended.

- Respect each child's privacy. Learn never to ask questions that call for self-revelation or for sharing information that is not your concern. "Can I see a show of hands? How many of your parents went to Mass last Sunday?" is not a good line of questioning. Even though you are teaching about the Catholic faith, you do need to follow the same rules any teacher would with regard to your student's privacy.

- Realize that there is no perfect family. Even though the Church teaches the value of an intact family with a mother and a father in a permanent relationship, fewer and fewer families fit that criterion. Make sure that you never disparage families that may not be "perfect." It is better not to refer to families that do not fit the profile as broken, strange, bad, against Church teaching, or the like. (You can affirm that teaching without making judgments.) It is a good idea that you keep any judgments you have about a student's home situation to yourself.

- You can point to family life as wholesome and happy, but every family has problems. Some families may even be quite awful places to be. Unhappiness may come to the surface in your class. Be most careful not to draw attention to it.

- If you encounter serious problems, don't try to handle them yourself. Alcoholism, child abuse, drug addiction, and other problems may be present in the families of your students. Remember that you are not a therapist—you are a catechist. If you sense real problems, report what you observe to your director of religious education, to the principal, or to the pastor. They are all trained to deal with this kind of family situation.

- Develop the habit of physical and emotional distance from the students you minister to. Any signs of affection should be group signs. No matter how in need of affection a student may seem, for your sake and for the student's sake do not single him or her out for special attention. Note: you may be required to take a class and be certified in the proper behavior you need to have when you are with the students you teach.

- Do develop the habit of maintaining contact with the families of your students through correspondence, take-home activities, or even an occasional phone call. Simple gestures like these are a lesson in themselves—reminding the students and families alike of the relationship between the formal catechesis in the parish and the family, the home church.

A Plan

1 Do a personal inventory on what habits you already have that might be put to practical use in your catechetical ministry. You can do an inventory of what habits you think you need to develop, too.

2 Sign up for a teaching methods course.

3 Find a mentor. Almost every parish program has a few seasoned veterans or at least some volunteers who are also classroom teachers. Ask one of those veterans to help you develop some good catechetical habits.

4 Be active in the life of the parish.

Prayerful Reflection

Read Saint Paul's Epistle to the Romans 12:3–17. Consider how these words can motivate you to develop good and practical catechetical habits. Write a summary of your reflection.

____

____

____

GLOSSARY

This glossary is a ready reference of Catholic terms. You will find the glossary that is located at the end of the *Catechism of the Catholic Church* to have more complete definitions. Nonetheless, these quick definitions will be helpful and handy.

A

ABSOLUTION The words by which the priest pardons the sins of the penitent.

ACOLYTE Another name for Mass server; one who assists the priest at the altar.

ADORATION Acknowledgment of God as Creator, Savior, Lord, and Master.

ADVENT The season that prepares for the coming of Christ at Christmas.

ALTAR The center and focal point of a church; the table at which the sacrifice of the Mass is celebrated.

AMBO The reading stand where the Scripture is read at Mass.

ANGEL A spiritual creature that glorifies God and serves God as a messenger.

ANNUNCIATION The visit of the Archangel Gabriel to the Virgin Mary to tell her that she was to become God's Mother.

APOSTLE One of the twelve original followers of Jesus.

APOSTLES' CREED A statement of the Christian faith developed from the baptismal creed.

ASCENSION The entry of Jesus into heaven.

ASSUMPTION The dogma that recognizes that the Blessed Virgin Mary was taken up body and soul into heaven.

B

BAPTISM The first of the sacraments by which original sin and all other sin is taken away. By the pouring of water and the invocation of the Blessed Trinity, baptism gives new life in Christ and makes one a member of the Church.

BEATITUDES The teachings of Jesus in the Sermon on the Mount on the meaning and way to true happiness (Matthew 5:1–12 or Luke 6:20–23).

BIBLE Sacred Scripture—inspired by the Holy Spirit. The Bible contains the Old and New Testaments.

BISHOP One who has received the fullness of the sacrament of holy orders. He is the chief shepherd of a diocese.

C

CANON OF THE MASS The Eucharistic Prayer—a prayer of thanksgiving and consecration.

CARDINAL VIRTUES The four pivotal moral virtues of prudence, justice, fortitude, and temperance.

CATECHESIS The education of children, young people, and adults in the faith of the Church.

CATECHISM A popular summary of Catholic teaching.

CATECHUMEN A person who is preparing for baptism.

CATHOLIC One of the four marks of the Church.

CHARITY The theological virtue by which one loves God above all things and one's neighbor as oneself.

CHRIST From the Greek translation of the Hebrew Messiah ("anointed"), a name proper to Jesus as the one who completely fulfilled the divine mission of prophet, priest, and king; the anointed one.

CHURCH The name given to the assembly of the People of God.

COMMUNION OF SAINTS The unity in Christ of all the redeemed—those on earth and those who have died; another name for the Church.

CONFESSION The telling of one's sins to a priest in the sacrament of penance.

CONFIRMATION One of the sacraments of initiation that completes baptism with an outpouring of the gifts of the Holy Spirit that "confirm" the baptized and equip them for active participation in the life of the Church.

CONSCIENCE The capacity to evaluate the rightness or the wrongness of a human action and to choose the right action according to the law God has inscribed in our hearts.

CONTRITION Sincere sorrow for and hatred of sins that one has committed.

CROSS The instrument of execution on which Christ died. Catholics begin their prayers and actions with the Sign of the Cross.

D

DEACON A man who receives the sacrament of holy orders to assist the bishop and priests and provide service to the community.

DEVIL A fallen angel who sinned against God by refusing to accept his reign.

DOGMA The official, defined teachings of the Catholic Faith.

E

EASTER The feast of the resurrection—the greatest and oldest feast in the Christian calendar.

EASTERN CHURCHES Those churches of the East in union with Rome, but not using the Roman Rite. They include the Byzantine, Alexandrian, and Maronite churches—to name just a few.

ECUMENISM Promotion of the restoration of unity among all Christians.

EPIPHANY The feast of the "manifestation" of Jesus Christ to all people as the Messiah and Son of God.

EUCHARIST The sacrament of the Body and Blood of Jesus Christ—the sacramental action of thanksgiving traditionally known as the Mass.

F

FAITH A theological virtue that is both a gift and a human act by which the believer gives personal adherence to God and assents to the truth God has revealed.

FRUITS OF THE HOLY SPIRIT The perfections that the Holy Spirit forms in the faithful as the first fruits of eternal glory. The Church identifies twelve fruits of the Holy Spirit (*Catechism of the Catholic Church*, no. 1832).

G

GIFTS OF THE HOLY SPIRIT Attitudes that help the faithful follow the promptings of the Holy Spirit—wisdom, understanding, knowledge, counsel, piety, fortitude, and fear of the Lord.

GOSPEL The "good news" of God's mercy and love revealed in the life, death, and resurrection of Jesus Christ. Four books of the New Testament— Matthew, Mark, Luke, and John.

GRACE The free gift that God gives so that people can respond to God's call and become his adopted children; a share in God's life. Also, actual grace is the help God gives so that people may follow his will.

H

HAIL MARY The popular prayer to the Blessed Mother that praises her and asks for her intercession.

HEAVEN Eternal life with God.

HELL The state of self-exclusion from communion with God reserved for those who freely refuse to be converted from sin—even to death.

HOLY DAYS OF OBLIGATION
The principal feasts of the year
(including Sundays) on which
participation at Mass is required.

HOMILY Preaching by an
ordained minister on the Scriptures
proclaimed in the liturgy.

I

IMMACULATE CONCEPTION
The dogma that from the very
moment of her conception,
Mary was free of original sin.

INCARNATION The fact that
the Son of God assumed human
nature and became man to save
all from sin and death.

INFALLIBILITY The gift of the
Holy Spirit to the Church whereby
the pope and the bishops in union
with him can proclaim a doctrine
for the belief of the faithful.

J

JESUS CHRIST The eternal son
of God, who was born of the Virgin
Mary, suffered crucifixion and death,
rose from the dead, ascended into
heaven, and will come again in glory
to judge the living and the dead.

JUSTICE The moral virtue that
consists in the firm will to give what
is due to God and to neighbor.

L

LAITY The faithful who have been
fully initiated into the body of
Christ, but who have not received
the sacrament of holy orders.

LECTIONARY The official
book of readings for Mass
and other liturgical rites.

LENT Forty days of prayer and fasting
that begin with Ash Wednesday and
end at the Easter Triduum (beginning
on Holy Thursday evening).

LITURGY Originally meaning
"public work," it is the official
worship of the Church.

M

MAGISTERIUM The living
teaching office of the Church,
whose task it is to give an authentic
interpretation of the Word of God.

MARKS OF THE CHURCH The
four attributes of the Church
mentioned in the creed—one,
holy, catholic, and apostolic.

MASS The Eucharist or principal
sacramental celebration of the
Church. The word comes from
the Latin word *missa* meaning
"sending forth" or "mission."

MERCY The loving kindness or
compassion shown to one who offends.

MORTAL SIN A grave infraction of the law of God that destroys the divine life in the soul of the sinner. For a sin to be mortal, three conditions must be met—grave matter, full knowledge of the evil of the act, and full consent of the will.

N

NEW COVENANT The new order established by God in Jesus Christ; the new Law of the Gospel.

NICENE CREED The profession of faith, common to the Christian churches of the East and West.

O

OLD COVENANT The old order that God established with his chosen people, Israel.

ORIGINAL SIN The sin by which the first human beings disobeyed God, choosing instead to follow their own will; the consequent loss of grace. Original sin describes the fallen state of human nature.

P

PAPACY The supreme jurisdiction and ministry of the pope—the successor of Saint Peter and the Vicar of Christ.

PARABLES A characteristic feature of the teaching of Jesus; simple images or comparisons about the kingdom of God.

PASCHAL MYSTERY Christ's work of redemption—his passion, death, resurrection, and glorious ascension. The paschal mystery is celebrated in the liturgy of the Church.

PENANCE Conversion of the heart toward God and away from sin; also the sacrament of God's forgiveness.

PENTATEUCH The first five books of the Old Testament.

PRAYER The elevation of the mind and heart to God in praise, petition, thanksgiving, or intercession.

PRECEPTS OF THE CHURCH Positive laws made by Church authorities to guide the faithful to make a moral effort in their growth in the love of God and neighbor.

PRIEST One who has received the sacrament of holy orders to assist the bishop, to celebrate the Eucharist, forgive sins, and shepherd the faithful.

PSALTER The book of the psalms arranged for liturgical use.

R

RCIA The Rite of Christian Initiation of Adults—the catechumenate, or period of preparation for adults seeking to be baptized.

REVELATION
God's communication of himself
and of his divine plan through the
words of Scripture and by the saving
actions of his Son, Jesus Christ.

ROSARY A prayer in honor of
Mary that entails the repetition
of the Hail Mary, the Our Father,
and the Glory Be while meditating
on the mysteries of salvation.

S

SACRAMENT A sign of grace,
instituted by Christ and entrusted
to the Church. The sacraments
are seven in number—baptism,
confirmation, Eucharist, penance
or reconciliation, anointing of the
sick, holy orders, and matrimony.

SACRAMENTALS Sacred signs,
objects, prayers, or blessings
that, through the prayers of the
Church, have spiritual benefits.

SAINT The "holy one" who
leads a life in union with God
through the grace of Christ.

SALVATION The forgiveness of sins
and the restoration of friendship with
God. Salvation comes from God alone.

SANCTIFYING GRACE The grace
that heals human nature and gives a
share in the divine life of the Trinity.

T

TABERNACLE The receptacle in
the church where the Blessed
Sacrament is reserved for communion
for the sick and dying.

THEOLOGY The study of God
based on divine revelation.

TRADITION The living transmission of
the message of the gospel in the Church.

TRINITY The mystery of one God in
three Divine Persons—Father, Son,
and Holy Spirit. This inaccessible truth
is at the very root of the Church's
living faith as expressed in the creed.

V

VENIAL SIN Wrongful actions that do
not destroy the divine life in the soul.

VIRGIN BIRTH The conception of
Jesus in the womb of the Virgin Mary
by the power of the Holy Spirit.

VIRTUE The habitual and firm
disposition to do good.

VOCATION The calling or destiny
all have to love and serve God
and to follow his will in life.

Y

YAHWEH (YHWH) The personal
name of the God of Israel as revealed
to Moses, meaning "I am who I am."